MILITARY MACHINES

SUBMARINES

BY CHARLES MARLIN

WWW.APEXEDITIONS.COM

Copyright © 2025 by Apex Editions, Mendota Heights, MN 55120. All rights reserved. No part of this book may be reproduced or utilized in any form or by any means without written permission from the publisher.

Apex is distributed by North Star Editions:
sales@northstareditions.com | 888-417-0195

Produced for Apex by Red Line Editorial.

Photographs ©: Mass Communication Specialist 1st Class Daniel Hinton/US Navy/DVIDS, cover; General Dynamics/US Navy/US Sixth Fleet, 1, 14–15; Mass Communication Specialist 2nd Class David A. Brandenburg/US Navy/DVIDS, 4–5; Mass Communication Specialist 2nd Class Alex Perlman/US Navy/DVIDS, 7, 8–9, 29; GL Archive/Alamy, 10–11; Smith Archive/Alamy, 12; US Navy, 13; Shutterstock Images, 16–17, 27; Chief Mass Communication Specialist Ahron Arendes/US Navy/DVIDS, 18; Mass Communication Specialist 1st Class Ronald Gutridge/US Navy/US Strategic Command, 19; Petty Officer 1st Class Ryan McLearnon/US Navy/DVIDS, 20–21; Mass Communication Specialist Seaman Darek Leary/US Navy/DVIDS, 22–23; NB/ROD/Alamy, 24–25; Mass Communication Specialist 1st Class Andrea Perez/US Navy/DVIDS, 26

Library of Congress Control Number: 2024941298

ISBN
979-8-89250-340-2 (hardcover)
979-8-89250-378-5 (paperback)
979-8-89250-450-8 (ebook pdf)
979-8-89250-416-4 (hosted ebook)

Printed in the United States of America
Mankato, MN
012025

NOTE TO PARENTS AND EDUCATORS

Apex books are designed to build literacy skills in striving readers. Exciting, high-interest content attracts and holds readers' attention. The text is carefully leveled to allow students to achieve success quickly. Additional features, such as bolded glossary words for difficult terms, help build comprehension.

CHAPTER 1
UNDERWATER ATTACK 4

CHAPTER 2
HISTORY 10

CHAPTER 3
DIFFERENT JOBS 16

CHAPTER 4
CONTROLLING A SUB 22

COMPREHENSION QUESTIONS • 28
GLOSSARY • 30
TO LEARN MORE • 31
ABOUT THE AUTHOR • 31
INDEX • 32

CHAPTER 1

UNDERWATER ATTACK

A submarine sneaks into a dark bay. Enemy ships watch the sea above. But the sub is underwater. It passes by unseen. It drifts close to the shore.

Many ships can move faster than submarines. So, subs must sneak up on enemies.

Inside the sub, a team of Navy SEALs put on dive gear. They sit in a large room. It fills with water. Then a hatch opens. The SEALs swim out into the ocean.

LOCKOUT TRUNKS

Some submarines have lockout trunks. These rooms fill with water. The **pressure** inside matches the pressure of the ocean. Then divers can open a hatch to swim out.

Lockout trunks let divers leave subs underwater. Otherwise, hatches can open only above water.

The SEALs sneak to shore for a surprise attack. Then they return to the sub. It has been hiding at the bottom of the bay.

Divers use oxygen tanks to breathe underwater.

FAST FACT
SEALs are skilled soldiers. They complete tasks on land and in water.

CHAPTER 2

History

People first used submarines for battle in the American Revolutionary War (1775–1783). Early subs were small and made from wood.

People turned hand cranks to power early subs.

In the 1800s, people began making metal submarines. Submarines became stronger. They began using **torpedoes**. By World War I (1914–1918), all major navies had submarines.

In World War I, German submarines shot torpedoes at British and US ships in the Atlantic Ocean.

During World War II (1939–1945), U-boats sank hundreds of ships carrying oil or other supplies.

 U-BOATS

Germany made submarines called U-boats in the 1900s. U-boats were faster than other subs. They could dive deeper, too. They took down many supply ships.

13

Submarines started using **nuclear** power in the 1950s. Nuclear subs can move quickly. And they can stay underwater for long periods.

FAST FACT

By the 2020s, nuclear submarines could stay underwater for a few months at a time.

Modern subs reach speeds of up to 40 miles per hour (64 km/h).

CHAPTER 3

DIFFERENT JOBS

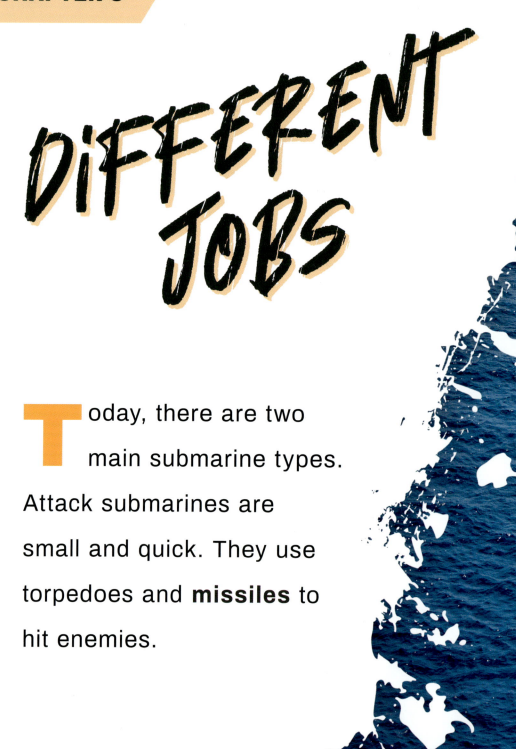

Today, there are two main submarine types. Attack submarines are small and quick. They use torpedoes and **missiles** to hit enemies.

Attack submarines are about 360 feet (110 m) long.

Ballistic missile submarines carry nuclear **weapons**. These subs travel along coasts. Their missiles can hit things up to 4,000 miles (6,400 km) away.

Some ballistic missile submarines are 560 feet (170 m) long.

Submarine missiles can be huge. Some weigh more than 65 tons (59 metric tons).

FIRING MISSILES

Submarines fire missiles from below water. But missiles fly through the air. Blasts of steam launch them out of the water. Then the missiles use rockets to fly.

Submarines complete many **missions**. Some guard ships. Some lay **mines**. Other subs sneak into enemy waters to spy. Soldiers can use the information to plan attacks.

Submarines may travel with ships in groups called fleets.

FAST FACT
A sail sticks up from the top of each sub. This part looks like a tower. It holds many sensors.

CHAPTER 4

CONTROLLING A SUB

Near the surface, a submarine uses **GPS** to **navigate**. Crew members use periscopes to see. These tools help crews look around. Most of the sub stays hidden underwater.

Periscopes stick up from the top of submarines. Some periscopes stretch to be 60 feet (18 m) tall.

Below water, a sub uses sensors to track its location. Sonar is one example. This tool uses sound waves to find where objects are.

Sonar shows what it finds on a screen. Crew members watch for danger.

SONAR TYPES

Subs use two kinds of sonar. Passive sonar collects sounds from nearby things. Active sonar sends out sound waves. The waves hit objects and bounce back. They show what's around the sub.

Submarines need large crews. Some crew members steer the sub. Some fire weapons. Other crew members do repairs. They keep the sub working.

Submarine crews usually stay at sea for three to six months at a time.

Most crew members sleep in tiny bunks. The beds are often stacked in threes.

Fast Fact
More than 100 sailors work on one sub.

27

COMPREHENSION QUESTIONS

Write your answers on a separate piece of paper.

1. Write a few sentences describing the two main types of submarines.

2. Would you like to work on a submarine? Why or why not?

3. When did submarines begin using nuclear power?

    A. the 1700s
    B. the 1800s
    C. the 1950s

4. Why might submarines shoot missiles from underwater?

    A. so the subs can make as much noise as possible
    B. so the subs can stay hidden while firing
    C. so the missiles will not explode

5. What does **launch** mean in this book?

*Submarines fire missiles from below water. But missiles fly through the air. Blasts of steam **launch** them out of the water.*

- **A.** send into the air
- **B.** stay under the water
- **C.** dive very deep

6. What does **repairs** mean in this book?

*Other crew members do **repairs**. They keep the sub working.*

- **A.** times when ships sink
- **B.** tries to break something
- **C.** work to fix something

Answer key on page 32.

GLOSSARY

GPS

A system that uses satellites to figure out locations.

mines

Devices that are placed underwater and explode if bumped.

missiles

Objects that are shot or launched as weapons.

missions

Tasks or plans with specific goals.

navigate

To find one's location and plan which way to go.

nuclear

Having to do with parts of the tiny bits of matter called atoms.

pressure

A force that pushes against something.

torpedoes

Underwater missiles.

weapons

Things that are used to cause harm.

BOOKS

London, Martha. *Military Submarines*. Minneapolis: Abdo Publishing, 2020.

Schuh, Mari. *Military Ships and Submarines*. North Mankato, MN: Capstone Publishing, 2023.

Storm, Ashley. *US Navy*. Mendota Heights, MN: Apex Editions, 2023.

ONLINE RESOURCES

Visit **www.apexeditions.com** to find links and resources related to this title.

ABOUT THE AUTHOR

Charles Marlin is an author, editor, and avid cyclist. He lives in rural Iowa.

INDEX

A
American Revolutionary War, 10
attack submarines, 16

B
ballistic missile submarines, 18

C
crews, 22, 26

G
Germany, 13

L
lockout trunks, 6

M
mines, 20
missiles, 16, 18–19

N
Navy SEALs, 6, 8–9

P
periscopes, 22
pressure, 6

S
sonar, 24–25

T
torpedoes, 12, 16

U
U-boats, 13

W
World War I, 12

ANSWER KEY:
1. Answers will vary; 2. Answers will vary; 3. C; 4. B; 5. A; 6. C